First published 2008 by order of the Tate Trustees
by Tate Publishing, a division of Tate Enterprises Ltd,
Millbank, London SW1P 4RG
www.tate.org.uk/publishing

A catalogue record for this book is available from the British Library

ISBN-10: 1854377795
ISBN-13: 9781854377791

Distributed in the United States and Canada by Harry N.Abrams inc.,New York

Library of Congress number 2008922618

David Goodman and Zoe Miller
www.millergoodman.com
www.silence.co.uk

Printed in China by Imago

SHAPE

By David Goodman & Zoe Miller

every has a

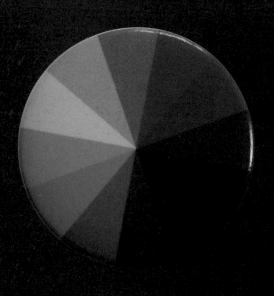

Circles are round.

Circles fit inside circles.

Circles look the same whichever way you turn them.

circle

Look inside these circles what can you see?

Can you find some circles and semi-circles here?

oval

A triangle has three straight sides and three corners.

Same-sized triangles fit
together closely side by side.

Diamonds and squares made from triangles

Count the triangles on these trees.

All
triangles
have three sides,
but they can be different shapes.

Match these triangles
with those on the right.

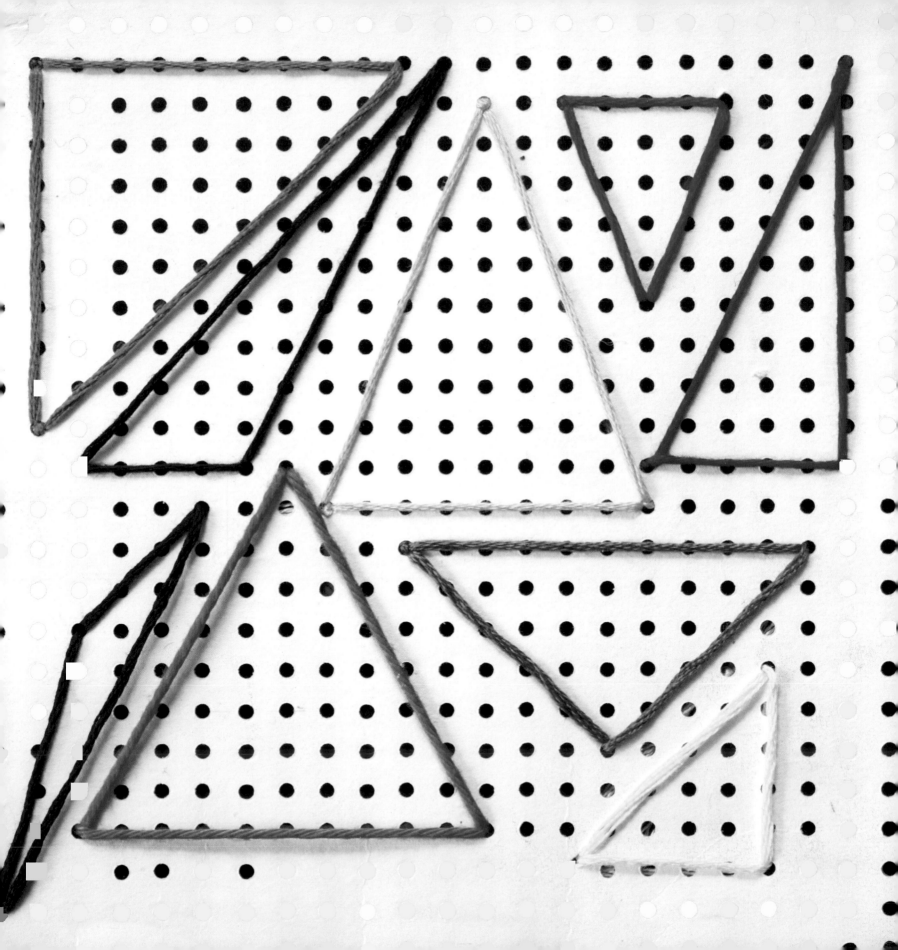

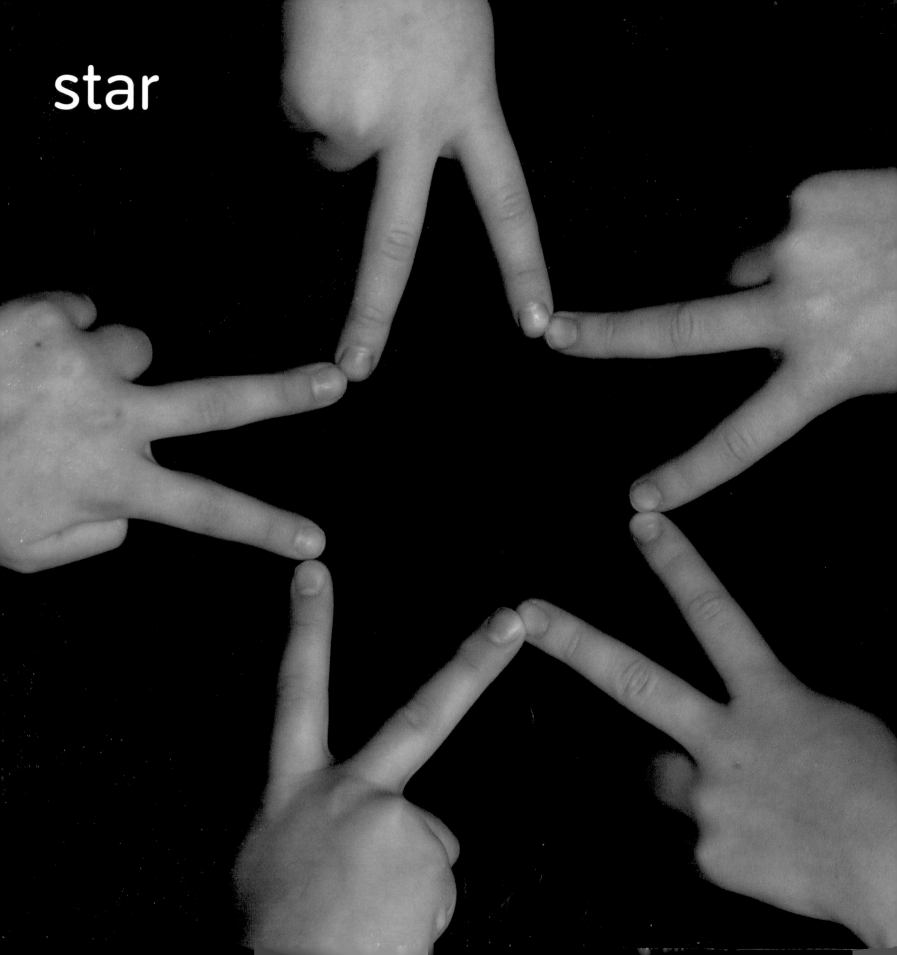

star

Triangles can also make stars.

Look at these stars in the dark.

A square has four straight sides.

The corners are all the same size.

I AM SQUARE

A square has four corners.

The sides are all the same length.

Look around you to find some squares.

A tangram is a square
cut into seven pieces, like this.
The pieces can be arranged
into all sorts of new shapes…

Trace the tangram above on
to some card. Cut out the
pieces. Have fun making
shapes with them.

Spot the rectangles in this town.

rectangle

A rectangle has two long sides

and two shorter sides.

You can make the most wonderful pictures with shapes

When both halves of a shape match exactly, this is called symmetry.

symmetr

Put a mirror across any of these flowers.
What do you notice?

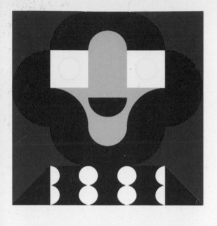

These shapes have been used to make faces.

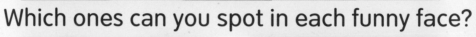

Which ones can you spot in each funny face?

PRINTING WITH SHAPES

Can you find shapes
in the picture puzzle
that match the white
ones above?

Can you tell what animals these are from their outlines?

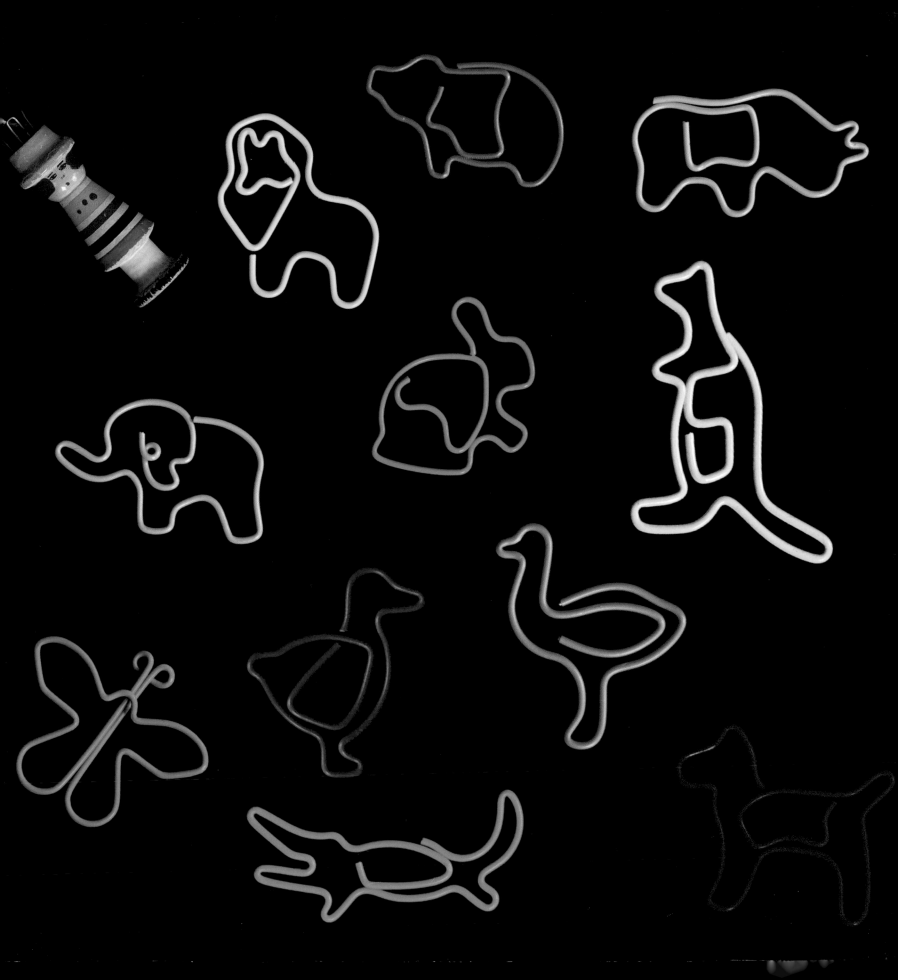

LETTERS ARE
MADE OUT OF
SHAPES

....so are faces.

Make a fish mobile

1 Trace or copy these fish onto card.
2 Cut them out. Colour both sides.
3 Pierce a hole on the top and bottom
   of each fish.
4 Thread cotton through both holes,
   knotting it between each fish.
5 Hang the fish from the ceiling
   or a window.

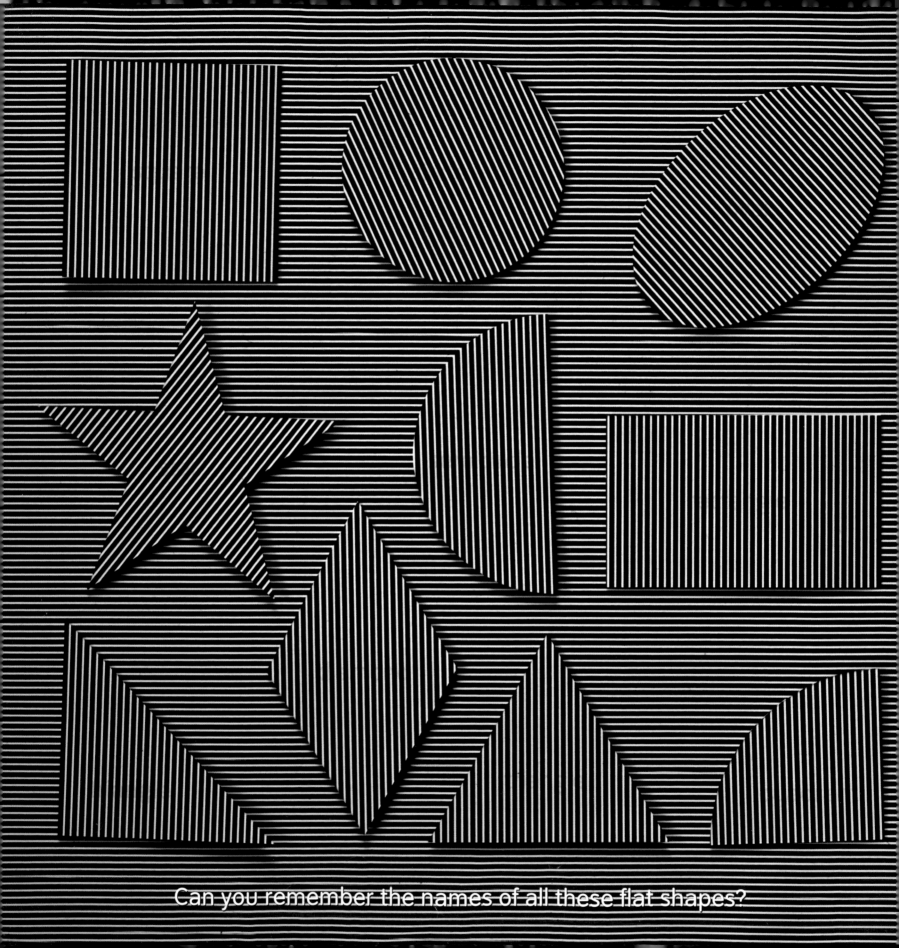

Can you remember the names of all these flat shapes?

You can use flat shapes to build solid shapes.

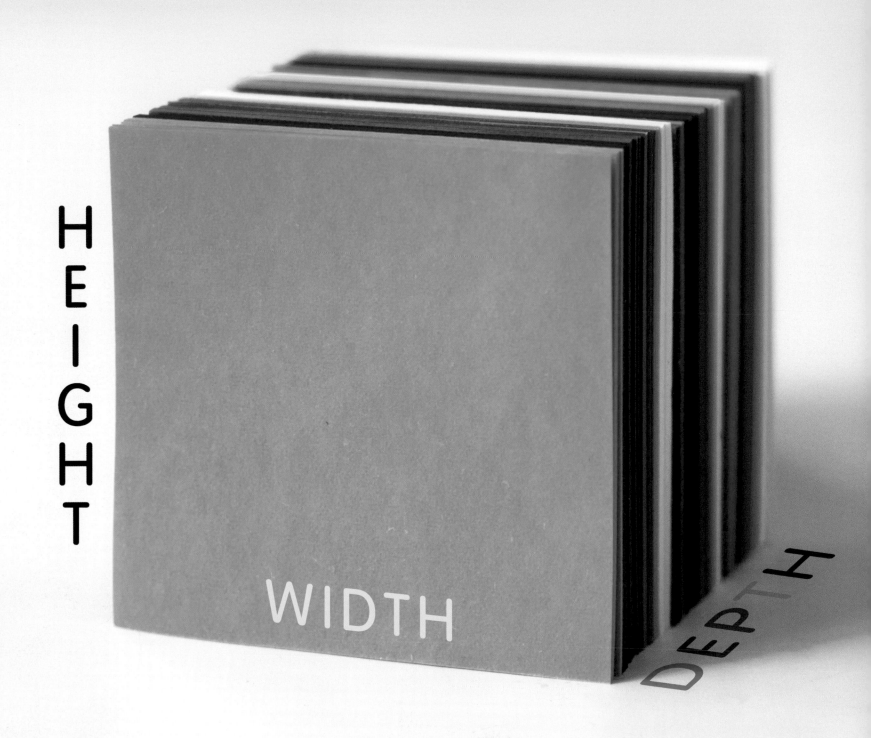

HEIGHT

WIDTH

DEPTH

A solid shape has height, width and depth. Solid shapes are called 3D.

A sphere is round. It has no flat or straight sides.

Some spheres are solid. Others are hollow.

sphere

cone

cylinder

A cube has six square sides.

A cube looks the same from all sides.

The sides of a cube are all the same size.

pyramid

Can you spot some pyramids, cones, cylinders and cubes in this town?

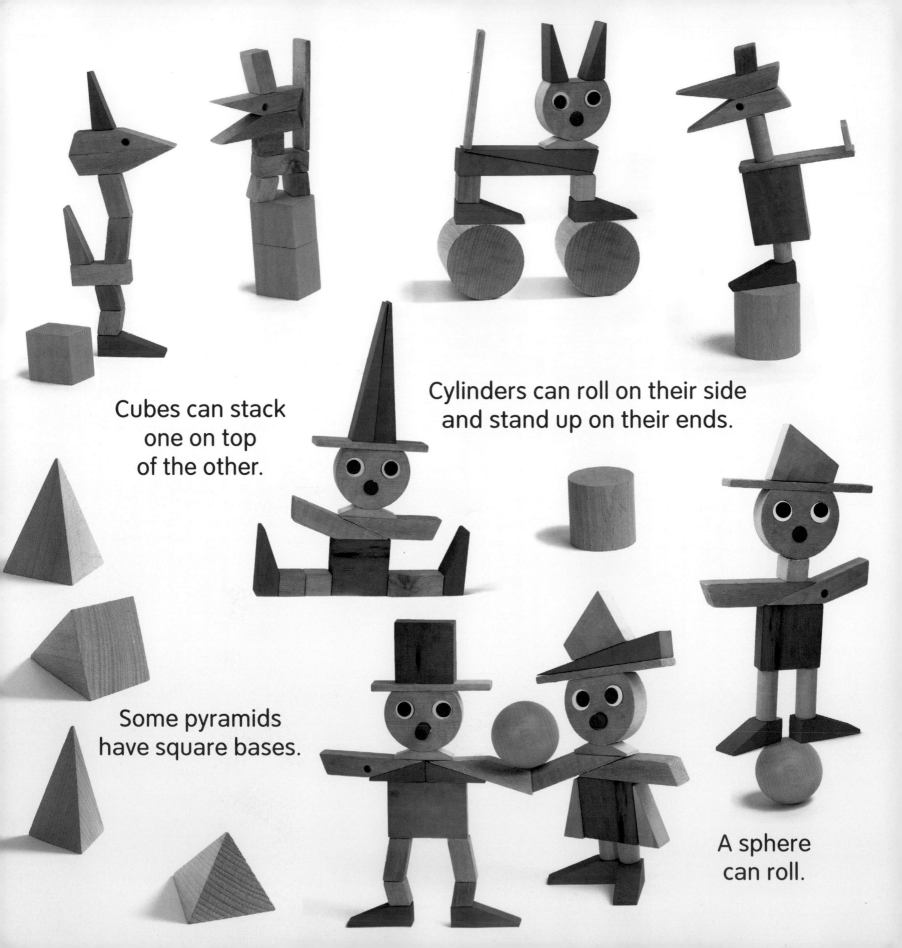

Cubes can stack one on top of the other.

Cylinders can roll on their side and stand up on their ends.

Some pyramids have square bases.

A sphere can roll.

a big thankyou

Finlay Arenz, Moose Azim, Fiona Bruce, Dylan Cutler, Sam & Emily Fysh, Harry Fuller, David Goldberg, Hannah Goodman, Michelle Goodman, Amalie & Erin Holbrook, Jeff Kazimir, Miri Felicia Layzell-Calder, Joni & Lola Leach, Ella Dede Lovatt, Helena Lawrence, Kitty Mellor, Erin Mcdermott, Eve Miller, Brian Miller, Saul Miller, Alex @ Workshops for the Imagination, Grace Hogben, Kitty Quinton, Kamran & Soloman-Shah Amin, Franscesca Stevelman, Ossie Stockman, Dylan Poucher, Blake Azim-Smith, Ruth Thomson, Isla Whittaker, Katvig clothing, Apple, Adobe, Nikon & Illy Coffee.